ANIMAL SUPERPOWERS

BY CHRISTOPHER HERNANDEZ

SCHOLASTIC INC.

NEW YORK   TORONTO

SYDNEY   MEXICO CITY   NEW

For Edward and Eddie, the best sidekicks a brother could ask for.

Photo credits:
Front Cover: Falcon: © Arco Images GmbH/Alamy; Cheetah: © Mark Beckwith/Shutterstock; Gecko: © Alexander Chaikin/Shutterstock; Bat: © McDonald Wildlife Photography/Animals Animals

Title page: © Alexander Chaikin/Shutterstock; Page 2: © McDonald Wildlife Photography/Animals Animals; Page 3: © imagebroker.net/SuperStock; Page 4: © Mark Beckwith/Shutterstock; Page 5: © Arco Images GmbH/Alamy; Page 6: © Alexander Chaikin/Shutterstock; Page 7: top © Emanuele Biggi, bottom © Luigi Masella/Getty Images; Page 8: © Michael Durham/Minden Pictures; Page 9: © McDonald Wildlife Photography/Animals Animals; Page 10: © Chesapeake Images/Shutterstock; Page 11: © imagebroker.net/SuperStock; Page 12: © imagebroker.net/SuperStock; Page 13: left © Minden Pictures/SuperStock, right © Minden Pictures/SuperStock; Page 14: © efendy/Shutterstock; Page 15: © Nick Stubbs/Shutterstock; Page 16: © David Shen/SeaPics; Page 17: top right © R. Andrew Odum/Getty Images, middle right © blickwinkel/Alamy, bottom © Minden Pictures/SuperStock; Page 18: © Kendall McMinimy/Getty Images; Page 19: © Minden Pictures/SuperStock; Page 20: © Scott Linstead/Foto Natura/Minden Pictures; Page 21: © Scott Linstead/Foto Natura/Minden Pictures; Page 22: © Masa Ushioda/SeaPics; Page 23: © David B Fleetham/SeaPics; Page 24: © Satoshi Kuribayashi/Nature Production/Minden Pictures; Page 25: © Handout/Reuters/Corbis; Page 26: © Bruce Davidson/naturepl.com; Page 27: top © David Paynter/Getty Images; bottom © Daryl Balfour/Getty Images; Page 28: © WansfordPhoto/Shutterstock; Page 29: © Alessandrozocc/Dreamstime; Page 30: left © Jeff Rotman/SeaPics, right © David Shen/SeaPics; Page 31: top © Robert Yin/SeaPics, left middle © Michael Aw/SeaPics, left right © Richard Herrmann/SeaPics, bottom left © Lori Breeden/SeaPics

ISBN 978-0-545-41564-4

10 9 8 7 6 5 4 3 2 1   12 13 14 15 16 17/0

Printed in the U.S.A.   40
Design by Cheung Tai
First printing, August 2012

Do you think superheroes are the only ones that have superpowers?

THINK AGAIN!

What if you were so **strong** you could lift a bus? Or if you were so *FAST* you could outrun a speeding train?

Animals do impossible things like this every day. These animals may not be superheroes but they certainly have their very own

SUPERPOWERS!

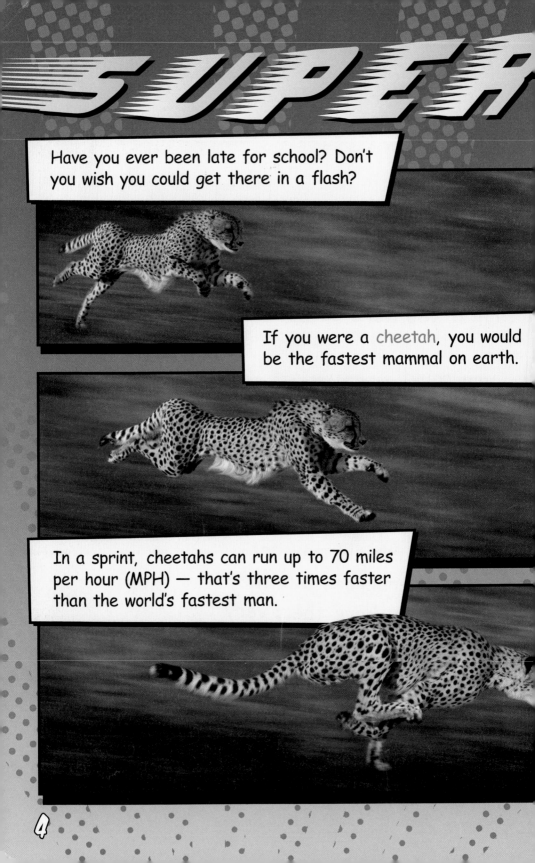

Have you ever been late for school? Don't you wish you could get there in a flash?

If you were a cheetah, you would be the fastest mammal on earth.

In a sprint, cheetahs can run up to 70 miles per hour (MPH) — that's three times faster than the world's fastest man.

SPEED

NOT SO FAST!

The fastest animal on the planet, however, is the peregrine falcon. When chasing their **prey**, these birds can reach up to an impressive 200 MPH in a single dive!

WALL CRAWLING

Your friendly neighborhood superhero isn't the only wall-crawler around. Many animals have the ability to walk on walls, but the gecko was clearly built for it.

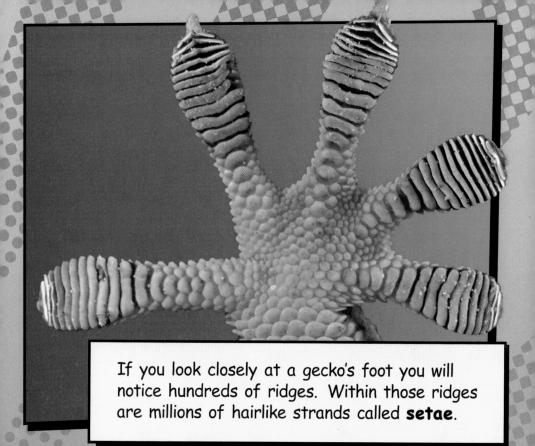

If you look closely at a gecko's foot you will notice hundreds of ridges. Within those ridges are millions of hairlike strands called **setae**.

When a gecko climbs up a wall, each setae clings to the surface, giving it an amazing grip. The grip is so strong, the gecko can hold up its entire body with a single toe!

NIGHT

The only animals that can see in the darkest night are those that don't use their eyes at all — bats.

While **nocturnal** animals, like owls, have good vision at night, they cannot see in the pitch black. Bats, however, use **echolocation** to "see" their prey and find their way around.

VISION

Bats make high-pitched screeches and wait to hear their echoes. The time it takes for bats to hear the echo lets them know how far away an object is from them.

FLYING

Look! Up in the air! It's a bird! In fact, there are a lot of animals that can fly. The ruby-throated hummingbird is one of the best.

Hummingbirds are amazing fliers. They can fly backward, upside-down, and even hover in midair. This helps them drink the **nectar** from flowers, which can be very hard to reach.

The ruby-throated hummingbird is even more impressive because it can travel nearly 500 miles in a single flight. Every year this bird **migrates** to Central America over the Gulf of Mexico!

Ever wish you could leap buildings in a single bound? Or would you settle for just being able to slam dunk?

MEGA

Pumas can jump the highest of any animal. Standing roughly two feet tall and between three to six feet long, pumas can jump up an incredible 18 feet!

Fleas, however, are the best jumpers in the world. At only one-eighth of an inch long, fleas can jump almost eight inches high and 13 inches across. If you jumped that well, you'd be able to jump over a 20-story building and across four basketball courts!

SUPERST

Think the strongest animal on the planet is a large hulk like an elephant or a rhinoceros? Think again!

The strongest animal is actually no larger than a bar of soap. One **species** of dung beetle can pull over 1,100 times its own weight. If you were that strong, you would be able to pull around eight school buses!

HEALING

Healing is very important because even superheroes get hurt. Although every animal can heal, some have a superhealing ability.

When attacked by a **predator**, many lizards can sacrifice their tails instead of sticking around to defend themselves. Luckily, most lizards have the ability to **regenerate** their tails.

The most impressive healing ability belongs to the starfish, or sea star. Like lizards, starfish can grow replacement limbs. In fact, for some species, an entirely new starfish can grow from a single **severed** limb!

HEAT VISION

No, these animals cannot shoot heat rays from their eyes like some superheroes. Their heat vision is actually an ability to "see" heat.

Certain snakes known as pit vipers have the ability to detect small changes in the temperature of their environment. Pit vipers, like boa constrictors and pythons, use this ability to help them hunt their warm-blooded prey.

WATER

If you couldn't fly, how would you cross a lake to rescue someone or flee from a villain? Dash across, of course!

The basilisk lizard has the incredible ability to run on water, but not because it's superfast. This lizard is able to cross the water without sinking because of its webbed feet, large tail, and unique way of running.

Basilisk lizards use this ability to flee from predators, like snakes, that try to sneak up on them. If the lizard is interrupted mid-run, it will sink and resort to swimming to escape.

You're not going to like it when it's angry . . .
or when it's threatened.

SHAPE SH

At first glance, the porcupinefish looks like a small,
defenseless creature. However, if you look closely
you will see that it is covered with spines just like
a porcupine. When threatened, the fish will swallow
enough water or air to grow to several times its
normal size.

Then the spines, which normally lie flat, stand straight up. The porcupinefish transforms from a puny fish to a threatening ball of spikes!

Although they cannot throw fireballs or shoot lightning bolts, some animals do have their very own firepower.

FIREP

OWER

Unlike other winged insects, the bombardier beetle cannot quickly fly away from predators. So instead of flying, the beetle must fight. It can fire an explosive mixture of boiling hot liquid and gas—from its behind! Not only is the mixture hot enough to burn, it also stinks.

INDESTI

Unlike some superheroes, no animal is completely **indestructible**. However, some have very strong armor to protect themselves.

The pangolin has one of the best defenses. Almost its entire body is covered with sharp scales that act like a suit of armor. When a pangolin is threatened, it will roll itself into a tight ball that's nearly impossible to open. Some species are even capable of rolling away from extreme danger.

Ever been so embarrassed you wished you were invisible? Wouldn't it be fantastic if you could disappear?

Many animals use their **camouflage** to hide from predators. The glasswing butterfly does so by being almost completely invisible. Its wings, which make up most of its body, are almost entirely **transparent**. The glasswing butterfly's predators are in trouble. These see-through wings make the butterfly difficult to spot in its natural environment.

SECRET IDENTITY

No superhero is complete without a secret identity. Many animals have secret identities, too. They use their camouflage to look like fiercer animals and frighten away predators.

The mimic octopus is the master of disguises. It is the only animal known to **mimic** multiple species. Some scientists believe it is able to imitate up to 13 animals like sea snakes and lionfish.

GLOSSARY

Camouflage – A disguise used for blending in or hiding

Echolocation – The use of sound waves and their echoes to find objects

Indestructible – Unable to be destroyed

Migrate – To move from one place to another

Mimic – To imitate another animal in appearance and behavior

Nectar – A sweet liquid found in flowers

Nocturnal – An animal that is active at night

Predator – An animal that hunts other animals for food

Prey – An animal that is hunted for food

Regenerate – To grow or form again

Setae – Hairlike strands used for clinging to objects

Severed – Separated by cutting

Species – One of the groups into which animals can be divided

Transparent – Allowing light to pass through